SWANSEA
Simply the best!

By David Roberts

BRYNGOLD
BOOKS

First published in Great Britain in 2011
by Bryngold Books Ltd.,
100 Brynau Wood, Cimla,
Neath, South Wales SA11 3YQ.

www.bryngoldbooks.com

ISBN 978-1-905900-24-4

Typesetting, layout, editing and design
by Bryngold Books

**Printed and bound in Wales by
Gomer Press,
Llandysul, Ceredigion.**

Pictures wanted

You too, can play a part in recording the history of your area by contributing photographs to the next Swansea nostalgia book. Please telephone 01639 643961 or e-mail david.roberts@bryngoldbooks.com to discover the ways in which you can do this. We would be delighted to hear from you. All photographs, transparencies, negatives, black and white or colour, of people, places, events, streets, buildings, schooldays and sport are considered whatever their age, subject or format. They are all promptly returned. Also, if you have missed any of the previous 13 books then contact us now as some titles are still available.
You can also check out our website at
www.bryngoldbooks.com
for details of our other fascinating local nostalgia books.

Contents

Appreciation 4

Foreword 5

Proud Premier City 6

Street life 7

Familiar faces 45

District days 59

The performers 75

Younger days 85

Parties & parades 99

School report 113

On the move 129

Leisure time 141

Working ways 149

Mumbles & Gower 161

Sporting spirit 171

About the author

With a lifelong interest in local history, David Roberts has been compiling pictorial nostalgia books on Swansea and the surrounding area for nearly 15 years.

His publications are widely acknowledged as an invaluable contribution to the recording of the way people and places in the area once were.

A long time journalist and now publisher, he has witnessed at first hand many of the events and changes that his books remind us of. Many people eagerly await the annual culmination of his picture gathering to add to their collection yet another in a series of books that rank as one of the best social archives in the UK.

This is his 14th book on Swansea, where he worked for nearly three decades, alongside 13 others that feature Neath & Port Talbot. Together they mark not only a unique personal achievement, but also one of which the Swansea Bay area can be justifiably proud.

Appreciation

Many thanks to the Lord Mayor of Swansea, Councillor Ioan Richard, for his kind foreword to *Swansea - Simply the best!* It is a book which would not have been possible without the help and encouragement of many different people, not least those whose photographs from the past fill its pages.

We are particularly grateful this year for a significant contribution from Colin Riddle which delightfully mirrors the 1960s. Paul Smith also supplied many more reflecting the same decade. Others whose pictures appear include: Ray & Dorothy Lewis, Adeline Evans, Geinor & Peter Tremewan, Geoff Rees, the late Betty Key, Robert Wayne Davies, Barry Griffiths, Hugh Rees, Julie Jones, Phyllis Thomas, Steve Phillips, Alan Lloyd, Ashley Lovering, Barbara Griffiths, John Jones, Bernard Humphries, Christine Rix, Rev Roy Bevan, Clive Cockings, David and Eluned Govier, Colin Andrew, David Lile, Dennis Spinks, Dilys Frayne-Timothy, Gaye Mortali, Gloria Wilson, Hilary Evans, JV Hughes, Jodie Jones, Julie Cole, Alan Williams, Michael Jones, Bert Barton,

Delma Mainwaring, Noel Blows, Jean Evans, William Bateman, Rodger Green, A Hughes, Royston Morgan, Russ Thomas, Steve & Sandra McCulloch, TB Harris, Steve Davies, Terry & Joy Osborn, Trevor Davies, Hazel Rees, Vivian Davies, Les Saunders, Bob Cuthill, Alan Johns, Amanda Davies, Sarah Briggs, Mervyn & Betty Roberts, June Barret, Bill Morris, Dick Woolacott, Michael Jones, Hilary Isaac, Brian King, Madge Johns, John Wilks, Mrs JE Cloke, Charles Trew, John Murphy and Keith Taylor. Others without whose help the book would not have appeared include Gerald Gabb, Roy Kneath, David Beynon, John & Barbara Southard, Anthony Isaac and Neil Melbourne.

Finally, I must, as always, salute my wife Cheryl for her invaluable support in the publication of this and the many other books before it. Without that I am sure the task would have been far more difficult to achieve.

Foreword

I am delighted, as the first citizen of the City and County of Swansea to have the opportunity to contribute the foreword for this new publication by someone who has done so much down the past 14 years to provide an opportunity for so many people to play a part in recording the ordinary, everyday social history of the area.

As with all his books, David Roberts has managed to include images reflecting almost every aspect of life in and around the city in Swansea - Simply the best! In fact there will be few who turn its pages and fail to find some link with their own past.

This latest book brings to the fore another fine selection of photographs that capture our continually changing surroundings in days gone by and allows us to compare what we have now with what once may have been in its place.

The city centre street scenes and snapshots of the districts will revive memories for many. The sight of faces of people and friends that we once knew, but have perhaps been forgotten, will be a source of delight for others. By now, David has gathered many thousands of pictures into his eagerly awaited annual book and that in itself is no mean feat. Lots of these photographs would never have been seen by the majority of us were it not for the ever-growing, easily accessible album that these annual books have become and it is a tribute to the people of Swansea that they are prepared to share their photographic memories in this way.

Long may they continue to do this and long may David continue his labour of love in producing a series of books that allows us all to share them.

Swansea – Simply the best! The title says it all, both for the city and the book.

I am sure everyone will enjoy turning its pages. Congratulations David on yet another superb contribution to our city's life.

**Councillor Ioan Richard
Lord Mayor of the City
and County of Swansea**

Proud Premier city

Memories can manifest themselves in many ways as the variety of fascinating images in this book demonstrates. They capture much that has occurred down through the decades and evoke endless nostalgic thoughts.

Few memories however will rival those, much closer in time, of the day when Swansea City became the first club in Wales to win promotion to football's Premier League. The jubilant scenes and celebrations that followed are the stuff of pure nostalgia.

We salute the achievement of the Swans and the success they have brought not just for the club, but the city at large. *Swansea – Simply the best!* also includes views of the Vetch Field, where it all started and some exciting moments from past encounters.

It would be difficult to unearth anything else that has gripped the city in such a way or had such an impact for some time. Alongside such a high profile event there are others, less significant perhaps, but which will be recalled just as fondly by residents of the city, many of whom have contributed to *Swansea – simply the best!* In doing so they have helped to assemble a kaleidescope of Swansea's recent history from a people's perspective.

Alongside the successes, this year brought sad memories too. Not least the closure of Mumbles Pier for refurbishment and a transformation that will take it into the next century, along with much development around it. There are a number of images of the pier within this book and they will help to remind us of how it was when the wraps eventually come off the new.

So there, on the following pages, you have it, a reflection of the good and bad; happy and sad of everyday life in Wales' second city or better, its proud premier city by the sea.

**David Roberts,
September 2011.**

St Mary's Church and Boots the Chemist on Princess Way, early 1960s.

Street Life

The junction of High Street and College Street taken from the Woolworth cafeteria, opposite, mid-1960s.

The impressive frontage of the
Grosvenor Hotel and Cafe at
24 College Street, 1903.

Crowds throng the tram stop at the junction of St Helen's Road and Oystermouth Road, possibly on a bank Holiday, 1910. The Bay View Hotel is on the right. Passengers would alight from the tram here either to catch the nearby Mumbles Train at St Helen's station, or simply take a relaxing stroll along the promenade.

The Burrows Inn, Adelaide Street, early 1900s. In its day it would probably have been a popular local hostelry. The Evening Post offices and Morgan's Hotel are nearby now.

An early 1920s panorama of Swansea and its busy docklands including many long vanished landmarks. The construction of the Fabian Way dual carriageway and other developments, more latterly the advent of the SA1 development changed much of this scene forever.

An atmospheric view down a bustling High Street, early-1930s. The whole scene shows it was a hive of activity in those distant days.

The fruit market at Alexandra Road, early 1920s.

The Cameron Hotel, High Street,
early 1920s. Woolworth's store is to the
right. The company took over the Cameron
in 1938 and it was bombed during the
wartime bombing of 1941.

The shell of Dynevor School at the foot of Mount Pleasant looking up towards Townhill. The Swansea Grammar School building is visible in the middle distance, mid-1950s.

A post-war view of Swansea following clearance work after the devastation of the Three Nights' Blitz in 1941. The white building with the distinctive arches is on Castle Street and is little changed today. The steeple on the left is that of the bombed Holy Trinity Church and the neat terrace to its right is Belle VBue Street.

Construction work underway on The Kingsway as Swansea begins to rebuild after the Second World War, early 1950s. The Burlington Restaurant survived for many years and eventually ended up on the Kingsway. The decorative roof line of the Mond Building is on the left, behind it the twin towers of the Carlton Cinema, now Waterstone's and on the right is the rooftop of the Plaza Cinema with its familiar ventilators.

It was business as usual for Woolworth's in High Street, even without its upper storey as Swansea emerged from its wartime destruction, early 1950s. On the right, Castle Street still shows the scars of bombing while new roadways have been laid at College Street and Belle Vue Way though new building has yet to commence here. The gap in the buildings marks Welcome Lane.

Looking up Lower Union Street towards its junction with Oxford Street, 1950. Temporary market stalls on the left seem to be doing a brisk trade. On the right is the market and top left the twin towers of the former Carlton Cinema, now Waterstone's bookstore, can be seen.

Looking westward along The Kingsway, from the roundabout, early 1950s. The Dragon Hotel
has yet to be built on the right hand side along with many of the buildings that exist
on either side of the road today.

Ralph's second hand book shop, Alexandra Road, mid-1960s. It was popular with both
impoverished students and serious book lovers. Ralph Wishart also had a shop in Dillwyn Street.
The ornate railings in the middle of the road guarded the entrance to an underground public toilet.

Oystermouth Road undergoes widening after the removal of the track that once carried the Mumbles Railway, March 1968.

Oystermouth Road looking towards Mumbles, March 1968. The Mumbles Railway track has been removed, but St Helen's station can still be seen along with the Slip Bridge.

Looking up High Street from its junction with College Street and Welcome Lane, mid-1950s.

Onlookers observe the sorry fate of a Vauxhall Cresta car that became stuck in the sand at Swansea Beach and overwhelmed by the incoming tide, 1957.

This aerial picture taken about 1958 shows the extent of the damage caused by the Three Nights' Blitz of February, 1941. Among the first new buildings to be erected was the central fire station in Grove Place seen on the left. The car park to the left of Kingsway Circle became the site of the Dragon Hotel. Clifton Hill is on the top right of this view,

An atmospheric view of Dyfatty flats from what was Bridge Street, Greenhill, mid-1960s.

An odd juxtaposition of hoardings seen near the Vetch Field, late 1960s.

Removal work underway on a former landing stage near Weavers Mill on the River Tawe, early 1960s. The bridge in this picture was removed some years later and replaced by the current New Cut Bridge.

A panorama of Swansea and the docks from Pantycelyn Road, Townhill, August 1966.

A South Wales Transport double decker bus waits for passengers at its stand alongside St Mary's Church in the city centre, late 1960s.

The tortuous nature of the topography around Mount Pleasant and Constitution Hill is plainly visible in this late 1960s view of Cromwell Street.

Hewson Street, Mount Pleasant, seen from Terrace Road, 1976.

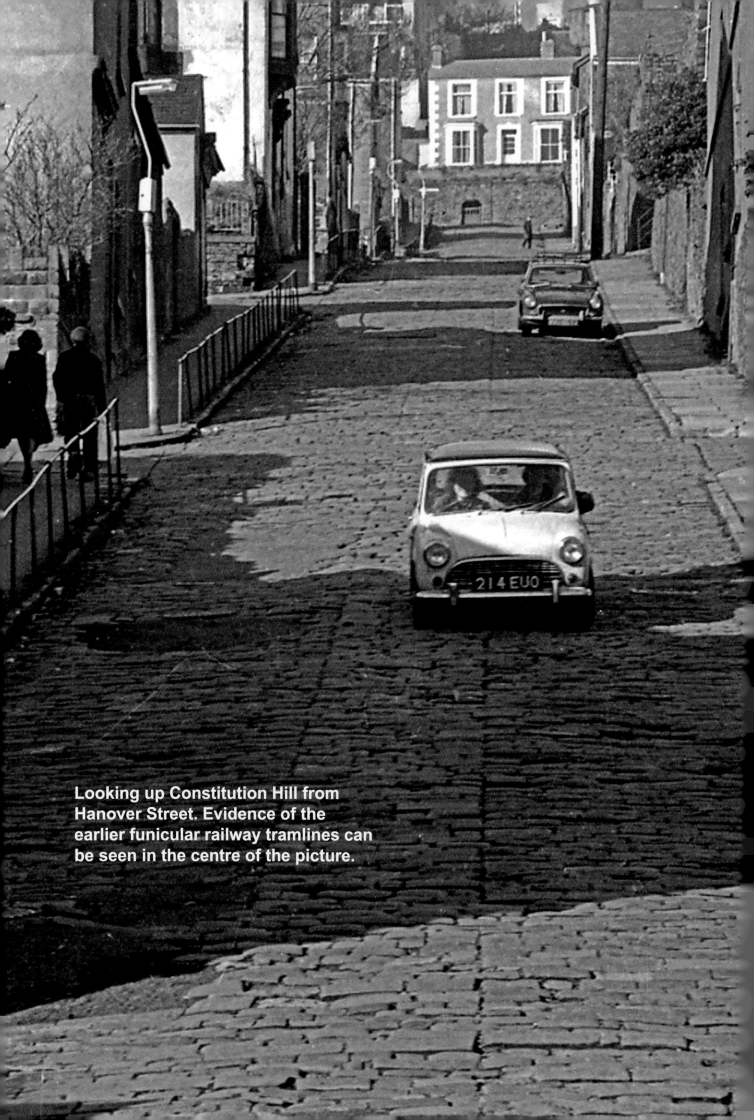

Looking up Constitution Hill from Hanover Street. Evidence of the earlier funicular railway tramlines can be seen in the centre of the picture.

Derelict land alongside the South Dock looking towards Townhill, early 1970s. The arches behind the rubble once carried the LMS Swansea Victoria railway line, while the grim exterior of Swansea Prison on Oystermouth Road can be seen behind them.

On the corner of Watkin Street and North Hill Road, Dyfatty, on an overcast Sunday in 1965. These well-dressed ladies must surely be heading for church or chapel.

This busy pedestrian thoroughfare, filled with flowers and greenery like the adjacent Kingsway roundabout was College Street as it appeared in 1969. The roundabout was later excavated for the creation of a pedestrian subway system. That was eventually filled in again to create the current traffic system.

Singleton Street bus station, with the Grand Theatre behind, 1976.

Council workmen struggle to clear blocked drains at the junction of Brynmill Lane and Oystermouth Road after heavy rain caused flooding, mid-1970s.

The twin towers of the former Carlton Cinema look down on Oxford Street, August 1976.

The Bay View Hotel at the junction of Oystermouth Road and St Helen's Road, 1976.

A view of Oystermouth Road dominated by the high wall of Swansea Prison, 1976. The Leisure Centre can be seen under construction in the background and part of Paxton Street, later demolished, on the right. The scene is almost unrecognisable today.

Some of the businesses that operated from the railway arches in Quay Parade that carried rail traffic across the centre of Swansea, 1972.

Looking along Singleton Street, towards the Guildhall, early 1970s.

Underneath the city's streets — Workmen in the original stone-built storm water drain in The Strand, July 1982.

Looking east along a busy Kingsway, festooned with Christmas decorations, 1985.

Looking down on Swansea Castle, the neighbouring Castle Cinema and Cobs Corner restaurant from the top of the BT tower, May 29, 1984.

Much change has occurred since this south westerly panorama of the city was captured on February 28, 1985. Landmarks include the former Post Office building in Wind Street, bottom right; The South Wales Evening Post building with the offices of Unifloc and the Powell Dyffryn building in front, middle left; Swansea Museum, centre and the former Maritime and Industrial Museum top right. The cranes in the distance signify the start of seafront housing development.

The now demolished stand at St Helen's rugby and cricket ground, July 26. 1989.

Derelict buildings at the top of Wind Street, viewed from Castle Gardens, 1995.

The Vetch Field before the demolition of the double decker stand, on the right, July 26, 1989.
Behind it is Swansea Prison; The Marriott Hotel, top left, is still under construction as is the Civic
Centre, top right.

Castle Gardens, was a green oasis in the city centre when this 1995 image was captured.
The central water feature has vanished and soon the entire garden followed suit.

The exterior of the Odeon Cinema, The Kingsway, and below, its foyer early 1990s.

These stone piers are the remains of the bridge that carried rail traffic in and out of the city from Neath and the docks. The Norwegian Church can be seen on the right while the railway bridge traversing Fabian Way was removed soon after this February 1985 picture was taken.

Scaffolding supports the bomb damaged remains of Swansea Grammar School, and as the view below shows, the interior was also in a ruinous state, November 1995.

The story of the Slip Bridge: Pictured above in February 2004, the spot it had occupied for almost 100 years; below, a month later, lying forlorn on the Recreation Ground where it underwent testing and some refurbishment and alongside, in its latest resting place on the prom where it was moved during August 2005.

The much loved David Evans department store shortly before demolition, May 2, 2007.

Extensive refurbishment work underway on the Patti Pavilion, January 26, 2008.

The Cardiff Arms public house, The Strand, 2000.

Youngsters having fun at Swansea's Winter Wonderland, November 2006.

How the city looked from the top of the seafront Meridian Tower, 2010. Seaview Primary School is on the centre skyline with Swansea Boys Club prominent at the end of the ridge on the right.

Work begins on the Meridian Tower block, Swansea Marina, November 11, 2007.

Concrete pumping underway during foundation work on the Salubrious Place hotel and leisure development, off Wind Street, late 1990s.

These women in Heol Hermas, Penlan, are about to start sandwich duty for the street party they held on Coronation Day, June 2, 1953.

Familiar Faces

Regulars at the Cardiff Arms public house, The Strand, 1972.

At 11:30 on Wednesday, September 3, 1947, Lieutenant Clifford Lloyd of Langland and Joan Hier of Sketty were married at St James's Church, Walter Road, surrounded by friends and family. The couple later held a reception at the Mackworth Hotel and soon after emigrated to Canada.

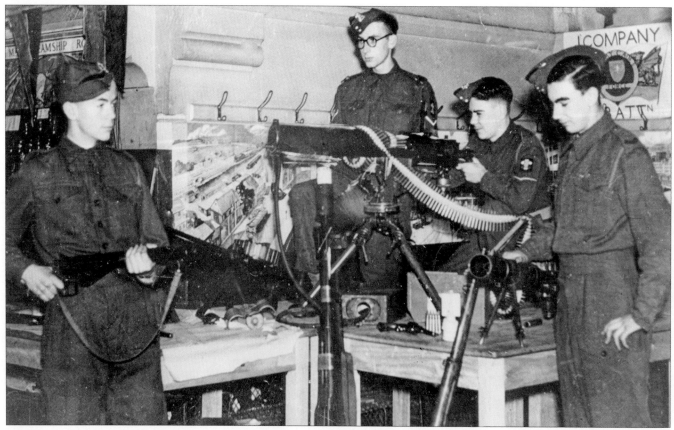

Swansea Army Cadets closely examining some wartime weaponry while manning a display at an exhibition in the city, 1944.

A group of men at Heol Hermas, Penlan, all dressed up during celebrations to salute the Coronation of Queen Elizabeth II, June 2, 1953.

The bride, groom and guests at a wedding reception at the Bush Hotel, High Street, May 1947.

**Youngsters from David Street, Cwmbwrla, during a visit
there from Swansea's Mayor and Mayoress, early 1950s.**

Three members of Pantygwydr
Baptist Church Guide Company,
Uplands, during a summer camp
at Penmaen, Gower, 1954.

Swansea members of the Army
Emergency Reserves about
to set off for their annual camp
in Dorset, summer 1953.

Salvation Army
officers from the High
Street Corps in High
Street, 1949.

Members of the committee of the Railmen's Club, Wind Street, late 1950s.

Adeline Athernought after her marriage to Michael Bury, 1946. She was a GI bride and moved to America.

A group of Waunarlwydd senior citizens at the village's welfare hall with the Mayor and Mayoress, Councillor and Mrs Wil George, mid-1950s.

A special civic presentation in the schoolroom of Mynyddbach Chapel, Treboeth, June 16, 1951.

A group of Swansea people at High Street station before setting off on a day out, early 1950s.

A group of Swansea senior citizens on a trip to Bournemouth, mid-1950s.

Members of the British Red Cross at Sketty Road, Uplands, during a demonstration of their skills, 1956.

A wedding party about to enjoy a reception at the Langland Bay Hotel, 1955.

Waunarlwydd senior citizens on the steps of the Mansion House when their local councillor Wil George became Mayor, 1959.

A presentation of a television to Morriston Hospital for use in the nurses' quarters, 1962.

A group of friends enjoying a night out at the Railmen's Club, Wind Street, mid-1960s.

Lord Mayor of Swansea, Grenville Phillips, with Councillor Alan Lloyd, Chairman of the Year of Literature, and their special guest, former US President, Jimmy Carter, 1995.

A surprise visit from a great artist. Lancashire painter LS Lowry, whose ward, Carol Anne Lowry, left, was then studying at Swansea College of Art, turned up unannounced in the summer of 1965, much to the delight of the painting students and their tutors.

The Welcome Inn, Mynyddbach, was the venue for this 50 year reunion of former members of New Siloh Chapel, Landore, 2004.

Members of the St Illtyd's Club darts team during a Silver Jubilee year celebration, 1995.

Participants in a Passion Play held in Swansea, in the grounds of St Mary's Church, mid-1970s.

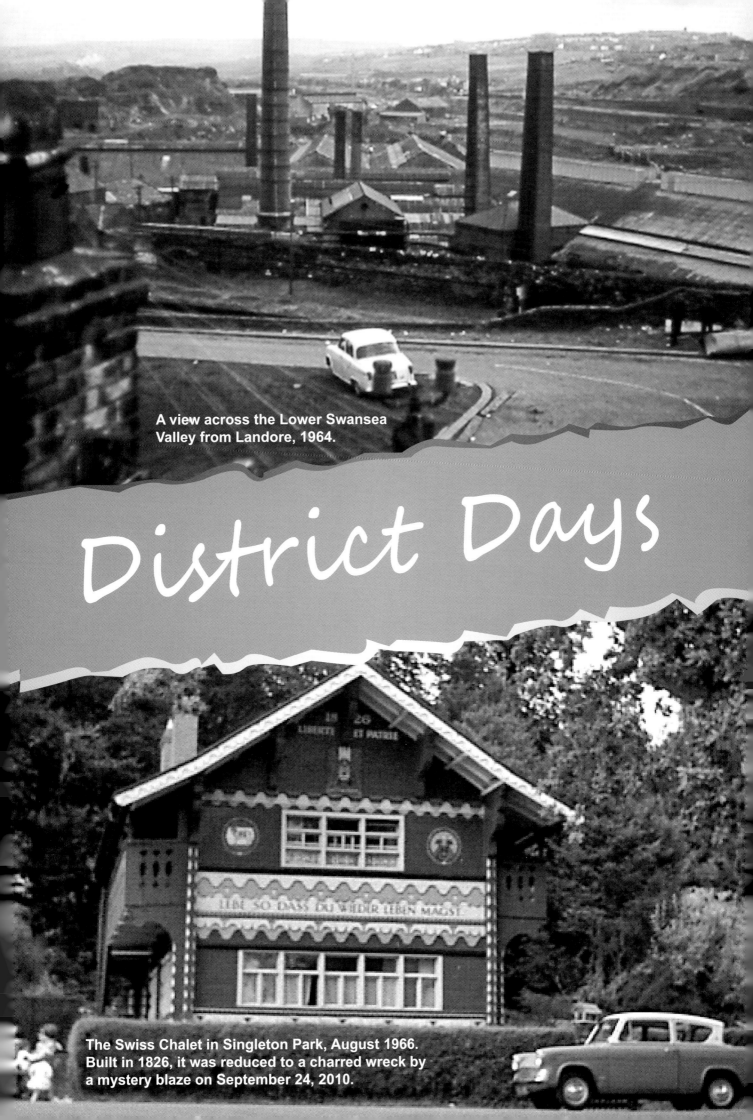

A view across the Lower Swansea Valley from Landore, 1964.

District Days

The Swiss Chalet in Singleton Park, August 1966.
Built in 1826, it was reduced to a charred wreck by
a mystery blaze on September 24, 2010.

The Mannesman tube works viewed from the north east, 1925. At the top is the Siemens steel works and behind the stacks the last two remaining blast furnaces that operated in Swansea are just visible. The high wall behind is the charging bank and on top of that, near the railway, you can make out the coke ovens. This site became part of the Richard Thomas & Baldwins steel works and then the Landore metal works. Now much of this scene has been redeveloped as Swansea Enterprise Park.

Ravenhill Park, it's attractive pavilion and ornate clock tower, summer 1947.

Looking across the River Tawe towards Hafod, early 1960s. The Pickford's storage building still dominates the skyline though in different ownership. The No.1 Shed was part of the Vivian & Sons copper works and was the shed that once housed the first Garrett type locomotives used in the UK.

Fabian Street, St Thomas, at its junction with Balaclava Street, 1963.

Greenhill Post Office on the crossroads at Carmarthen Road and Dyfatty Street, 1963. The buildings were later demolished and today the view is filled with a multi-lane traffic junction.

Fabian Street, St Thomas, between its junctions with Sebastopol Street and Balaclava Street, 1963. The building on the right is the Station Inn, which along with the majority of properties on the street was demolished to make way for construction of the Fabian Way dual carriageway. Fabians Bay Congregational Church, in the centre, still exists.

Looking eastwards from Ashleigh Road towards town along the former Swansea Victoria to Pontarddulais railway line, September 28, 1964.

The track of the Swansea Victoria railway line sweeps around the bay, September 28, 1964 shortly before its removal.

Looking eastwards from Blackpill along the former LMS railway line into Swansea Victoria station shortly before the track was removed, September 28, 1964.

A sand covered Swansea Bay railway station looking towards the Slip Bridge, June 4, 1965.

Sand on the tracks at Swansea Bay station, September 28, 1964.

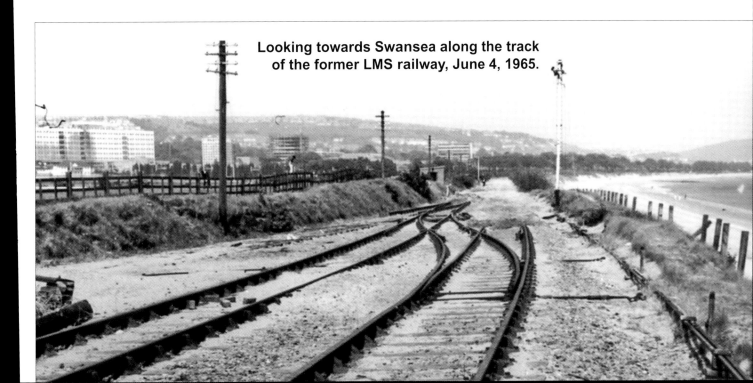
Looking towards Swansea along the track of the former LMS railway, June 4, 1965.

The derelict Siemens laboratory buildings with their distinctive chimneys near Landore railway viaduct, 1968. This was where Sir William Siemens experimented and perfected his open hearth furnace method of steelmaking during the 1860s.

These people have just crossed the Shrewsbury to Swansea Victoria railway line heading for Swansea Beach, near the Slip Bridge, June 4, 1965.

The Swansea Canal, alongside
Hafod Copperworks, 1965.

Britannia Hill,
Plasmarl, 1976.

A terrace of decaying houses overlooks the Swansea Canal at Neath Road, Landore, late 1960s.

A view of Davis Street, Plasmarl, 1976.

Looking up towards Davis Street, from Neath Road, Plasmarl, 1976.

Looking along Carmarthen Road towards Fforestfach Cross, early 1980s.

Looking down Siloh Road, towards
Neath Road, Landore, 1964.

Scaffolding surrounds the spire of
St Thomas Parish Church, June 1977.

The junction of Mumbles Road and Derwen
Fawr Road on January 10, 1982, after two days
of heavy snowfall.

Gwydr Mews, off Glanmor Road, Uplands, 1975.

Construction work underway on the new Loughor road bridge late 1980s.

The scene from Castle Graig looking towards Morfa, after heavy snow, early 1980s. This was before Morfa Athletic Stadium was built. The Liberty Stadium fills the view from here today.

The view north-east over the filled-in North Dock, across the River Tawe towards St Thomas and Kilvey Hill, February, 1985. The former St Thomas School is prominent in the background.

Cadle Infants School, Carmarthen Road, Fforestfach, 1990.

Demolition of Cadle Infants School, Carmarthen Road, Fforestfach, February, 1991.

Woodfield Street, Morriston, 1987.

Refurbishment of Pentrehafod School shortly before it was destroyed by fire,1987.

Gower Road, Sketty, near the entrance to Brynmill park, 2006.

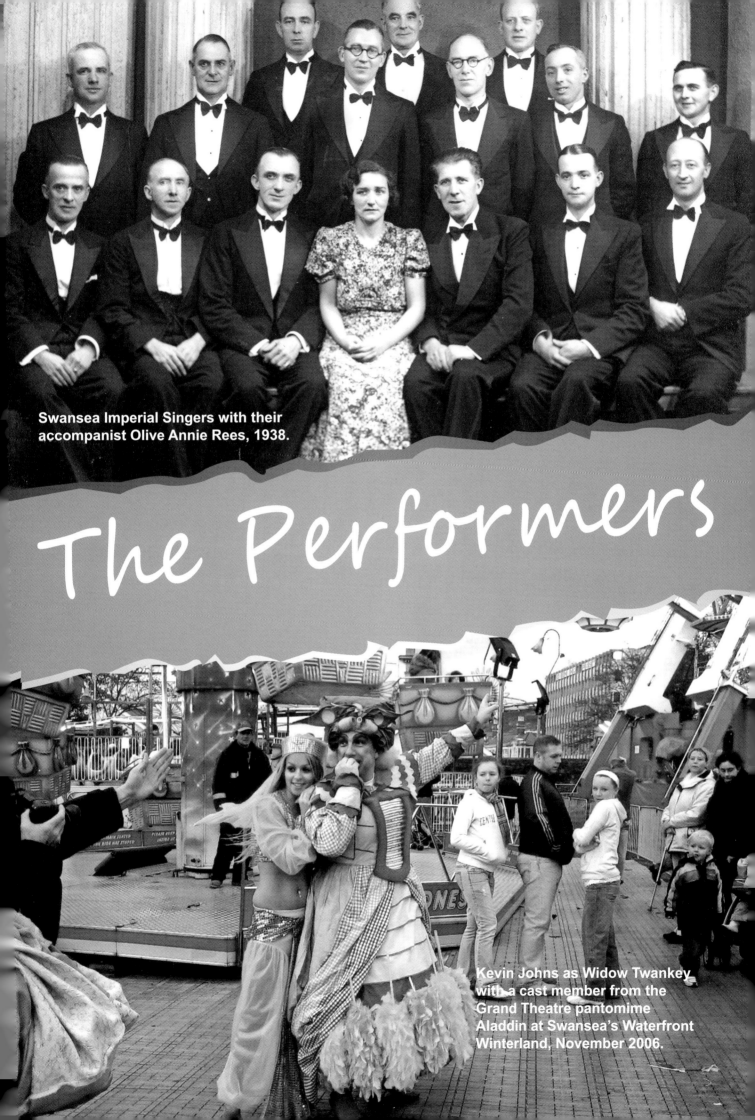

Swansea Imperial Singers with their accompanist Olive Annie Rees, 1938.

The Performers

Kevin Johns as Widow Twankey with a cast member from the Grand Theatre pantomime Aladdin at Swansea's Waterfront Winterland, November 2006.

The percussion band of Morriston Junior School, early 1930s.

Members of the band of Swansea High Street Corps of the Salvation Army during an open air parade, mid-1950s.

Glenys Shepherd, teacher and pianist for many years playing for one of the Nativity plays staged by Sunday School members at Terrace Road Chapel, early 1960s.

Popular Swansea Sound presenter Andy Lee, at his console in the station's Victoria Road, Gorseinon studios, 1979.

Participants in a Passion play staged by members of the congregation at St Michael's Church, Manselton, Easter 1970.

Art was not the only thing learned at Swansea Art College as these three budding musicians prove. Getting down to some serious practice in the 1960s are Geoff Waters, left, Colin Riddle, centre and Alvin Perkins on 12-string guitar.

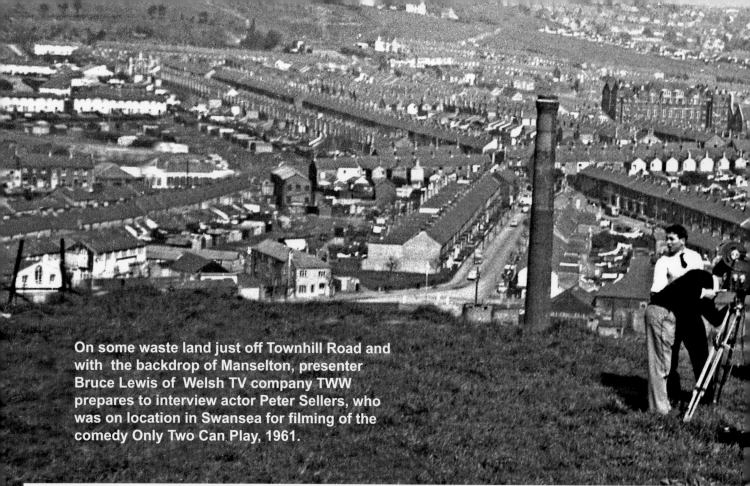

On some waste land just off Townhill Road and with the backdrop of Manselton, presenter Bruce Lewis of Welsh TV company TWW prepares to interview actor Peter Sellers, who was on location in Swansea for filming of the comedy Only Two Can Play, 1961.

A crowd gathers as actress Mai Zetterling leaves the BBC Alexandra Road sound studios after filming a scene for Only Two Can Play, summer 1961.

Actor Peter Sellers leaves the TWW television interview in the summer of 1961.

The choir and choirmaster at Hafod Junior Comprehensive School, 1975.

Some of the boys who were members of the Hazel Johnson Dance School, 1987.

Students of the West Glamorgan Dance Company, with tutors, at Dan-Y-Coed residential centre, Blackpill, Swansea, mid-1980s.

Cast members of Pentrehafod School's production of the musical Oliver, 1981.

The band of Swansea 215 Squadron Air Training Corps, 1952.

Members of Waunarlwydd Women's Institute on stage during a concert, 1968.

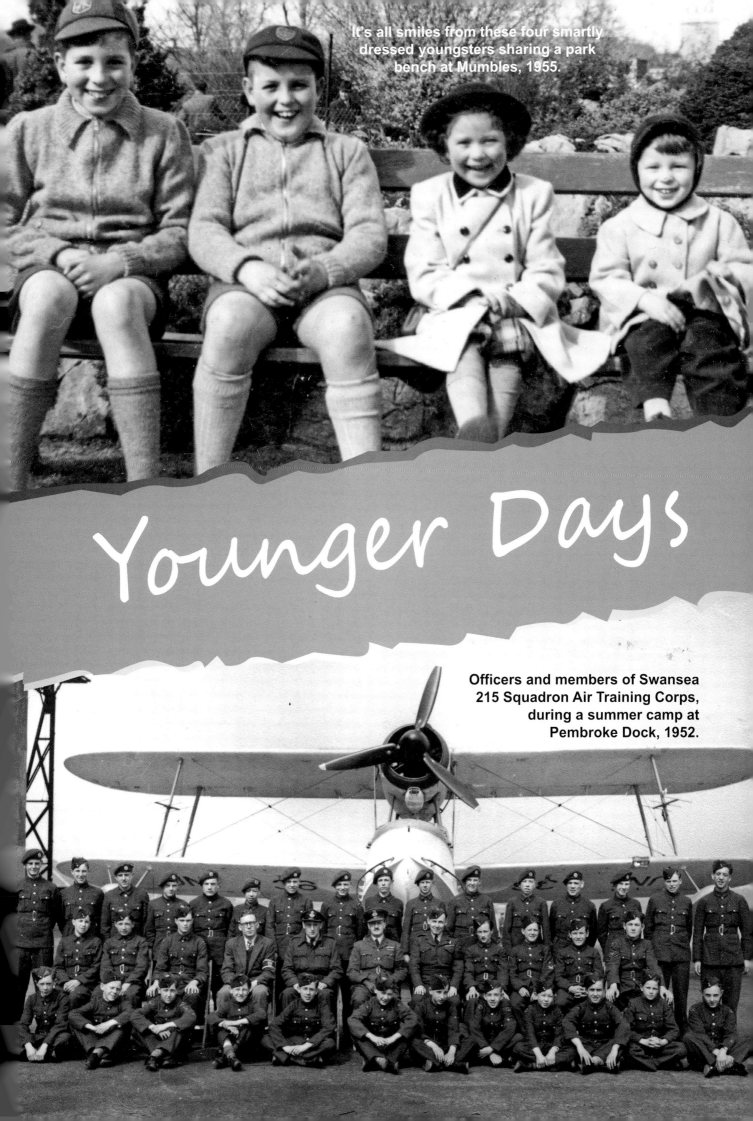

It's all smiles from these four smartly dressed youngsters sharing a park bench at Mumbles, 1955.

Younger Days

Officers and members of Swansea 215 Squadron Air Training Corps, during a summer camp at Pembroke Dock, 1952.

Tricycle fun, 1939-style!

A youngster gets a ride on her mum's bike at Seaview Terrace, Northill, 1946.

Madge Morris with some young pals in the garden of number 8 Glantawe Street, Morriston, 1931.

Children of Goronwy Road, Townhill, enjoy a trip to Caswell, 1947.

The Mayor of Swansea inspects Swansea Sea Rangers at their launch ceremony, June 1950.

Members of Swansea 215 Squadron Air Training Corps, 1952.

Cheeky Chops! This Manselton toddler was certainly making her point in 1961.

Having a swinging time in the playground at Blackpill in August 1966.

Three youngsters enjoy the sun at the gardens and play area Southend, Mumbles,1968.

A group of youngsters opposite Terrace Road Chapel, Whitsun 1957.

Members of the 16th Swansea St Gabriel's Scout Troop, Bryn Road, Brynmill, with their leaders outside the church, late 1940s.

A Sketty Brownie Pack with their leader at an event in Singleton Park, early 1950s.

Children of the Sunday School of Terrace Road Chapel enjoy an outing early 1960s.

A group of youngsters
and their parents enjoy
a summer afternoon at
Cwmdonkin Park, 1957.

Pictured outside Dai Thomas's barbers shop on Llansamlet Square in 1964, this could have been the occasion of the first haircut for the young lad in the pushchair!

A typical festive scene as these children open their presents, Christmas morning, 1965.

It seems it was cowboy — and girl — suits all round for these three, Christmas, 1965.

Santa puts in a special appearance at a Christmas party held for the children of employees at the Northgate sewing factory which operated from Hafod Church Hall, 1968.

These girls were members of Terrace Road Chapel's Sunday School, early 1970s.

Pantygwydr Church Brownie Pack, Uplands, 1980. Miss Eastman, their Brown Owl is in the centre at the back.

Children playing
outside their homes
in Cambrian
Place,1969.

Getting ready for
Bonfire Night at
Woodcote, Killay,
1974.

Snowman building time for this Gorwydd Road, Gowerton family, 1982.

Pupils from Mynyddbach School, all working towards their Bronze Duke of Edinburgh Awards with the WRVS, alongside two Army Cadets at an Award exhibition at Bishop Gore School, March 1980.

Children at Nelson Terrace Nursery School, 1975.

Clambering over a neighbour's car seems to have been good fun for these young residents of Cambrian Place, 1969.

Building a snowman at Maes Y Ffynon, Fforestfach, 1984.

SWANSEA – SIMPLY THE BEST!

A visit to Father Christmas was one of the highlights for these Morriston youngsters, Christmas time, 1990.

Snowman building time for this youngster at Milton Terrace, North Hill, 1992.

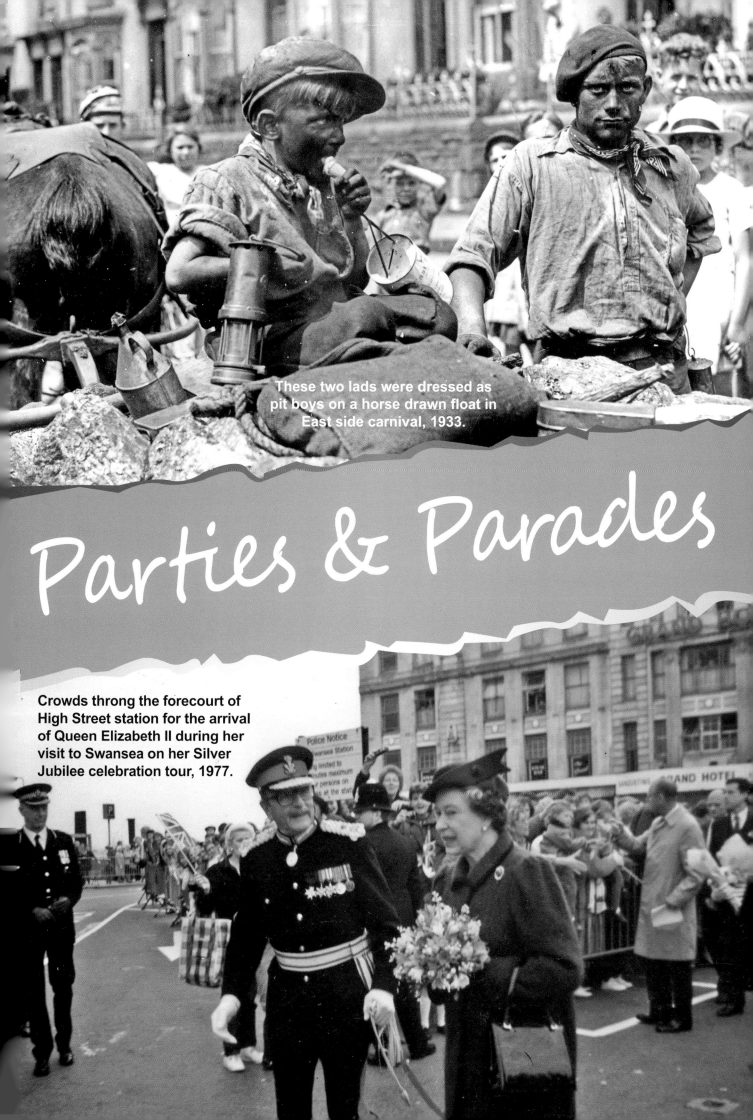

These two lads were dressed as pit boys on a horse drawn float in East side carnival, 1933.

Parties & Parades

Crowds throng the forecourt of High Street station for the arrival of Queen Elizabeth II during her visit to Swansea on her Silver Jubilee celebration tour, 1977.

The carnival queen's float heads up a procession as it passes the former Swansea Hospital and heads into Phillips Parade, late 1940s.

Members of the Swansea Womens' Junior Air Corps band lead a Battle of Britain Rememberance Parade along College Street and through the rubble strewn streets of blitzed Swansea, 1949.

Children of Heol Hermas, Penlan, prepare for the fancy dress parade during celebrations to mark the Coronation of Queen Elizabeth II, June 2, 1953.

Office staff of the Lewis Lewis department store, High Street at their annual staff dance, 1950. Miss Gwyneth Lewis is seated centre in the front row.

Three scenes from East side carnival, 1937. They show some of the participants, including the fairy and rosebud queens and their attendants.

A children's party at Waunarlwydd Welfare Hall to celebrate the Coronation of Queen Elizabeth II, June 2, 1953.

Women from the Premier Clothing and Supply Company's office at Alexandra Road, at a Christmas dinner and dance, late 1950s.

Waunarlwydd carnival queen and her attendants, 1953.

A group of Swansea and Port Talbot railway workers on a men's night out, 1964.

Swansea and Port Talbot railway workers and their partners on a Christmas night out, 1963.

Swansea University Rag Week was always an excuse for the Art College to go over the top with its float for the procession. This giant cow was the result of their efforts in 1964. It made its way down St Helen's Road towards Oystermouth Road and a close encounter with the Slip Bridge.

A group of Hodges Menswear employees enjoy a New Year's Eve party, 1965.

Members of staff of Littlewoods store during a staff dance, 1971.

A family group enjoys a night out at the Railmen's' Club, Wind Street, mid-1960s.

Bob and Lily Morse celebrate their golden wedding at St John's Church parish hall, Hafod, 1961.

Staff of the Hodge's Menswear factory, Fforestfach at the Maerdy Hotel, Gorseinon for a New Year party, 1971. The landlady is on the left, joining in the fun.

The St Elmo Avenue, St Thomas float at the East side Carnival, 1975.

Women dressed in traditional Welsh costume at Port Tennant awaiting the start of an East side carnival procession, mid-1970s. Behind them is an impressive line-up of carnival floats and in the distance the Carbon Black works.

A group of friends enjoy a drink at the Blackhills Grill, Fairwood Common, 1963.

Residents of Gloucester House, Gloucester Place, Swansea Marina, enjoy a party with all the trimmings to celebrate the 50th anniversary of VE Day, 1995.

Participants and onlookers in a Passion play seen in Castle Gardens, mid-1970s.

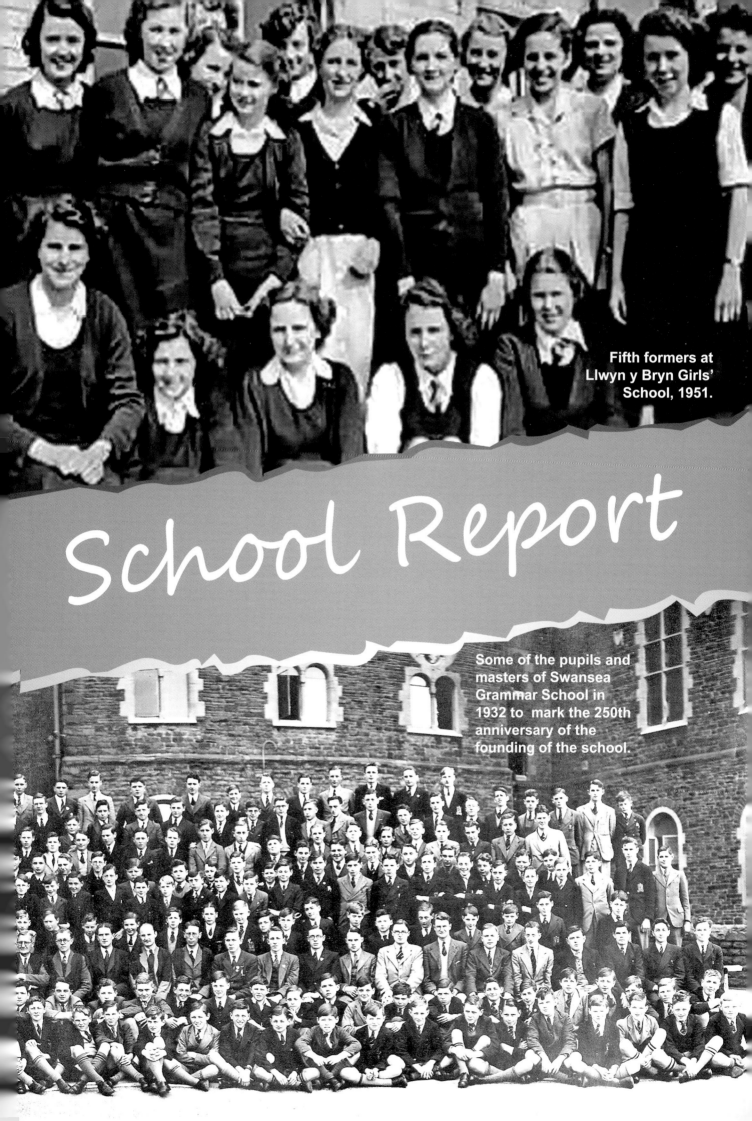

Fifth formers at Llwyn y Bryn Girls' School, 1951.

School Report

Some of the pupils and masters of Swansea Grammar School in 1932 to mark the 250th anniversary of the founding of the school.

These children, pictured with their teacher, attended Llangyfelach School, 1909.

Some of the first pupils to attend Glanmor School for Girls, 1922.

Girls of the lower sixth form at Llwyn y Bryn School, May 1952.

A group of pupils at Glanmor School for Girls, 1953.

Pupils of Bishop Gore Grammar School, 1953.

A class at Hendy School, with their teacher and head teacher, 1947.

The class of 37 — children that is! They were pupils at the then newly built Gwyrosydd Junior School, reached for many years by an unmade road between Penlan and Llangyfelach Road, 1954. Headmaster Mr Baton is on the right and the class teacher on the left.

A class at St Helen's Junior School with their teacher, 1965.

Some Townhill schoolgirls with student teachers, 1960.

Class 1A Dynevor School, with staff members, 1955-56.

Pupils of Form 3C at Dynevor School with their head teacher and teachers, 1955.

Some of the boys from Oxford Street Secondary School who took part in a school trip to Holland in 1957 dressed in Dutch national costume.

Art student Alan Perry working on a townscape viewed from the first floor of Swansea Art College, then in Alexandra Road, 1965.

Lunch break in the Antique Room, Swansea Art College, 1965.

Students at work in the painting studio of Swansea Art College, 1965.

A life painting exam in progress for Fine Arts finals at Swansea Art College, summer 1965.

Class J1, Waun Wen Junior School, 1970.

121

Brynhyfryd Junior School 11- plus class, 1968.

Three young Fforestfach schoolgirls dressed in Welsh costume, to celebrate St David's Day, 1981.

A group of year five girls at Pentrehafod Comprehensive School, 1978.

Pupils and teachers of Dumbarton House School, 1971.

These pupils of Gorseinon Infants School were dressed in traditional Welsh costume to celebrate St David's Day, 1974.

A class at Hafod Junior Comprehensive School, with their teacher, 1975.

Second year pupils in St Thomas Junior school, 1975. The teacher on the left is Eurfryn John, who was conductor of the Morriston Orpheus Choir from 1961- 69.

Class 1 at Brynhyfryd Junior school with their teacher Mrs Howells, 1980.

Girls of 6C Morriston Comprehensive School with their tutor, 1979.

MORRISTON
COMPREHENSIVE SCHOOL
SWANSEA
1979
FORM 6-C

**Pupils of Hafod Primary School with
their teacher and head teacher, 1983.
The teacher on the right is David Jenkins.**

A group of year five pupils at Pentrehafod Comprehensive School, 1978.

Pupils of form 2-1 at Brynhyfryd Junior School, 1981.

A class at the Stella Maris Convent School, Uplands, with their teacher, 1984.

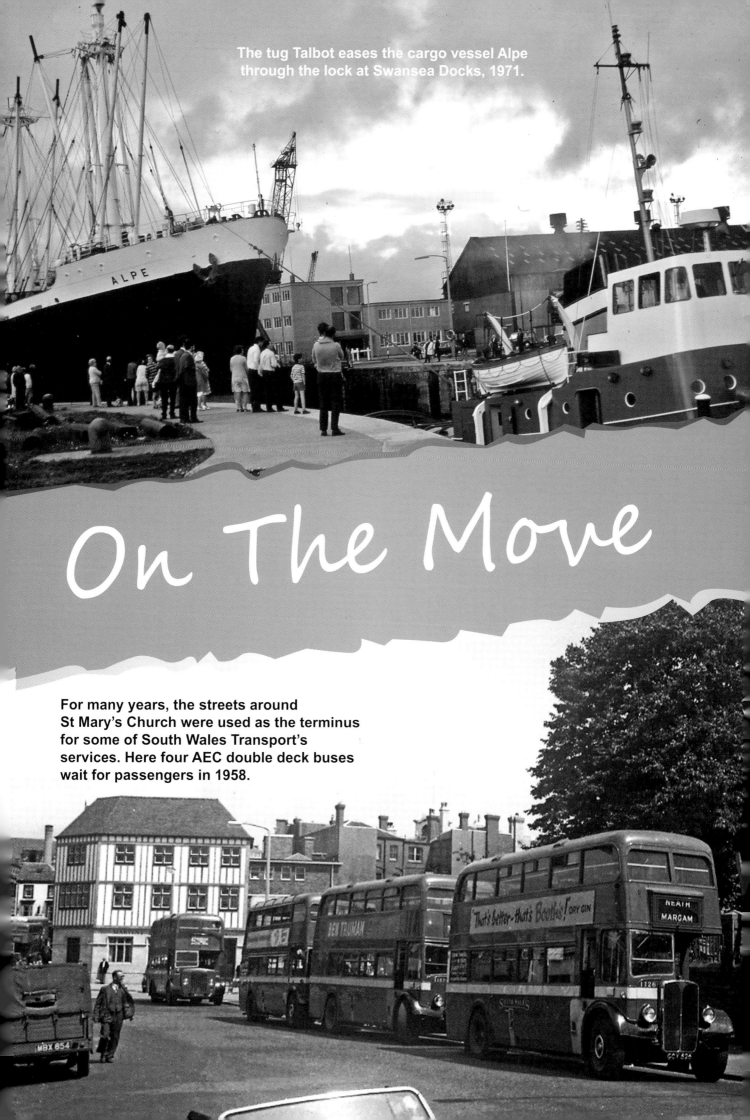

The tug Talbot eases the cargo vessel Alpe through the lock at Swansea Docks, 1971.

ALPE

On The Move

For many years, the streets around St Mary's Church were used as the terminus for some of South Wales Transport's services. Here four AEC double deck buses wait for passengers in 1958.

Loading underway at the coal hoists in King's Dock, 1912.

An impressive line up of delivery vans used by the Ben Evans department store with their drivers at Oystermouth Road, 1916.

A race horse bound for South America provided quite an attraction at Swansea Docks as it was loaded aboard the steam ship Clan Alpine, October 1954.

Upper Bank Station with its loco shed and coaling stage in the background.

Locomotive 47655 is being readied for its next tour of duty at the coaling stage of the Swansea Vale Railway's Upper Bank depot, mid-1950s. The line was by then part of British Railways.

In the late 1940s and early 1950s, this Morris bin lorry would have been a familiar sight on the streets of Swansea. Having reached the end of its days it lay rusting away, with other Swansea Council vehicles in a field near Clase in 1956.

The scene after two twin car Mumbles trains collided head on along a single-track stretch of line at Blackpill, summer 1959.

Lined up and loaded up, these
British Road Service vehicles await
their drivers at the company's
North Dock depot, Sunday
November 6, 1960.

Rows of lorries at British Road Services North Dock depot,
Sunday November 6, 1960.

Leyland Octopus lorries at the North Dock depot of British Road Service 1961. The building behind was part of Weaver's flour mill.

A small coaster at a coal hoist at Swansea Docks, mid-1960s.

A full lock at the entrance to Swansea Docks, mid-1980s.

A former United Welsh Bristol double decker, by then part of the South Wales Transport fleet, pulls out of Caer Street into Princess Way, 1972. Behind it the BT tower is under construction showing signs for the different floor levels.

A South Wales Transport bus company double decker in Gower Road, Sketty, on its way to Langland via Blackpill and Oystermouth, mid-1960s.

A British Rail diesel shunter pulls carriages through a train wash at Maliphant sidings, Hafod, July 1967.

A British Rail 'Stairway to Heaven' crossing look out point, Hafod, 1967.

STOP HERE UNTIL PERSON IN CHARGE GIVES AUTHORITY TO PASS OVER T E CROSSING

Four tugs owned by the Alexandra Towing Company moored at Swansea Docks, awaiting their next call to duty, 1989.

An unusual cargo being loaded aboard the Swansea to Cork ferry in the early 1990s. It was a number of giraffes bound for Ireland.

The old Mumbles lifeboat greets the arrival of a new replacement. The Ethel Anne Measures which had served the station well since 1985 leaves and is replaced by the vessel Babs and Agnes Robertson, July 16, 2006.

The steam tug Canning and the former Bristol Channel lightship Helwick, both floating exhibits alongside the former Maritime and Industrial Museum at the time seen in Swansea Dry Dock undergoing a regular inspection, late 1980s.

Work underway on the hull of a vessel berthed at Swansea Dry Dock, 1995.

A view across the city towards the mouth of the River Tawe and docks, with a Swansea to Cork ferry taking centre stage, mid-1990s.

The Swansea to Cork ferry, MV Superferry, leaving the mouth of the River Tawe bound for Ireland, August 4, 2004.

Four young women sporting the latest in ladies swimwear, in the sea at Oxwich, Gower, 1948.

Leisure Time

Boys from Bishop Gore School on a rugby trip to Twickenham, 1956.

SWANSEA – SIMPLY THE BEST!

Two young women push a smart Silver Cross pram along Oystermouth Road. Behind them, the Bay View Hotel, Mumbles train and Slip bridge are just visible, Easter, 1950.

A group of friends from Dunvant Senior School in London during the Festival of Britain, 1951.

A family enjoy a day at Caswell Bay, 1930.

Having fun at the water's edge, Oxwich, 1949.

Crowds enjoy a day out on the sand near the Slip, Swansea Beach, early 1950s.

A group of Swansea telephonists on a day out in Shrewsbury, 1960.

People enjoy the delights of the boating lake in Singleton Park, early 1960s.

A family outside their beach hut at Langland, 1959.

A party of men from the Raven public house, Penlan, all set for a day at the races, late 1960s.

Fifth form geography pupils at Penlan Multilateral School wait to board their Bryn Demery coaches in the school yard for a field trip to the Rhondda Valley, 1960.

Relaxing in deckchairs,
Langland early 1960s.

A coachload of people from
St Thomas during a trip to
Butlins Pwhelli, early 1970s.

A staff outing from the Lewis Lewis department store, High Street, 1968.

Members of the St Illtyd's Club, Port Tennant, all set for a rugby trip to Scotland, early 1970s.

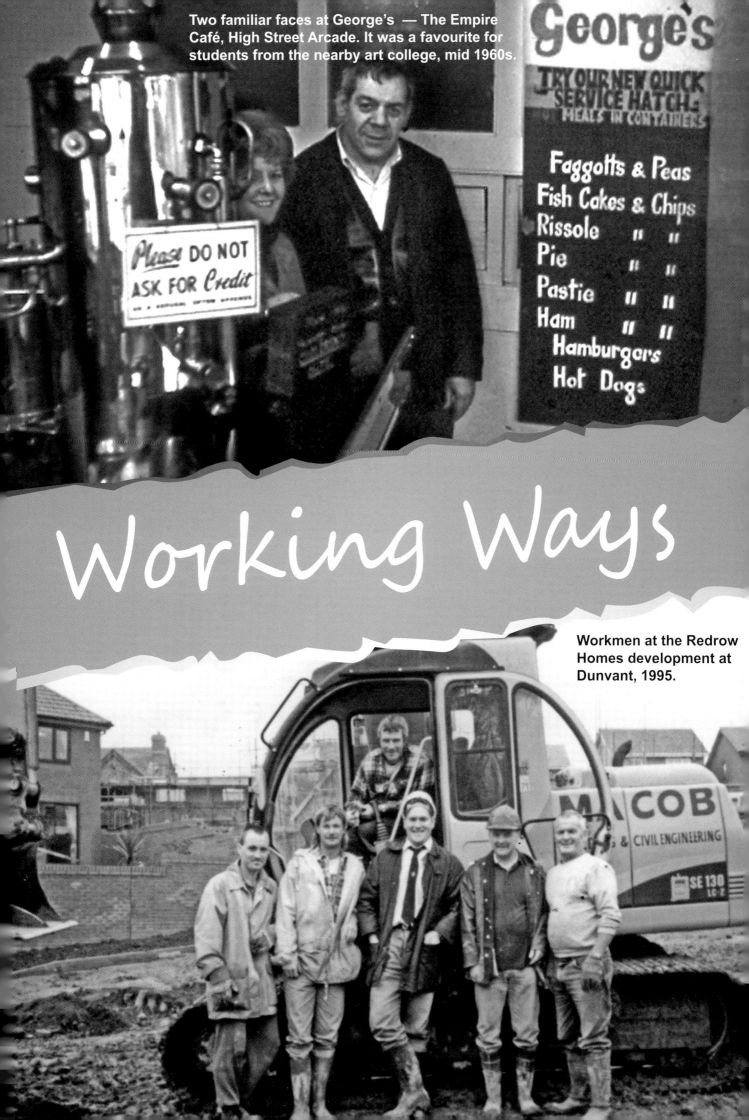

Two familiar faces at George's — The Empire Café, High Street Arcade. It was a favourite for students from the nearby art college, mid 1960s.

George's

TRY OUR NEW QUICK SERVICE HATCH.

MEALS IN CONTAINERS

Please DO NOT ASK FOR Credit

Faggotts & Peas
Fish Cakes & Chips
Rissole " "
Pie " "
Pastie " "
Ham " "
Hamburgers
Hot Dogs

Working Ways

Workmen at the Redrow Homes development at Dunvant, 1995.

M COB
& CIVIL ENGINEERING

SE 130

Members of Swansea County Borough Council's Health Department, who were based at the Guildhall, 1946.

Loading cargo at Kings Dock, 1960.

Railway staff who worked at Morriston station, 1930.

Members of the air raid warden team based at Landeg Street, Plasmarl, during the Second World War, 1940.

Workmen at Berthllwyd Colliery, between Gowerton and Penclawdd, 1930s.

Staff of the TJ Rice bakery, Gower Road, Sketty, in their Kardov flour overalls, late 1950s.

The Home Guard detachment formed from employees of the Cwmfelin Press and Fabricating Works of Richard Thomas and Baldwins Ltd. They were operational between April 13, 1942 and December 31, 1944.

Employees at Swansea Dry Dock, June 1951.

Workers at Swansea Docks, 1955.

Coach drivers of Daveys of Swansea at the North Shore car park, Blackpool, after conveying parties of Swansea people there, 1961.

Students and lecturers at the ICI Apprentices School, Landore, 1957.

South Wales Transport bus company signwriter, Gareth Davies, at work on an AEC Regent double decker painted in unfamiliar green to celebrate Swansea's elevation to city status, 1969.

A smiling park keeper at Cwmdonkin Park, Uplands, mid-1960s. Above, is the bell he used to ring around the park for many years at closing time.

Employees at Teddington Components, Pontarddulais, mid-1970s.

Two paper sellers on the corner of Alexandra Road and High Street, 1965. They were part of the scene here for many years.

Staff of Dynevor Comprehensive School, 1987.

Staff of the Kingsway office of the Western Mail newspaper enjoy an evening out, 1970.

A staff get together to mark the closure of the office at the Hafod depot of Unigate Dairies, July 1994. They festooned the office with Christmas decorations as they wouldn't be together in December to celebrate.

Memories of days when Swansea boasted its own newspaper press. This was the printing end of matters at the South Wales Evening Post shortly after it moved to Adelaide Street from its former site at Castle Bailey, 1967.

British Transport Docks Board mechanical engineers at Swansea Docks on the retirement of George Jones, chief mechanical foreman, April, 1971. He later emigrated to Sydney, Australia.

Colleagues gather for a presentation to a retiring fireman at Swansea Airport, late 1970s.

Building sand castles the easy way! This bucket loader driver was the envy of children watching him as he moved sand away from the sea wall along Oystermouth Road, early 1980s.

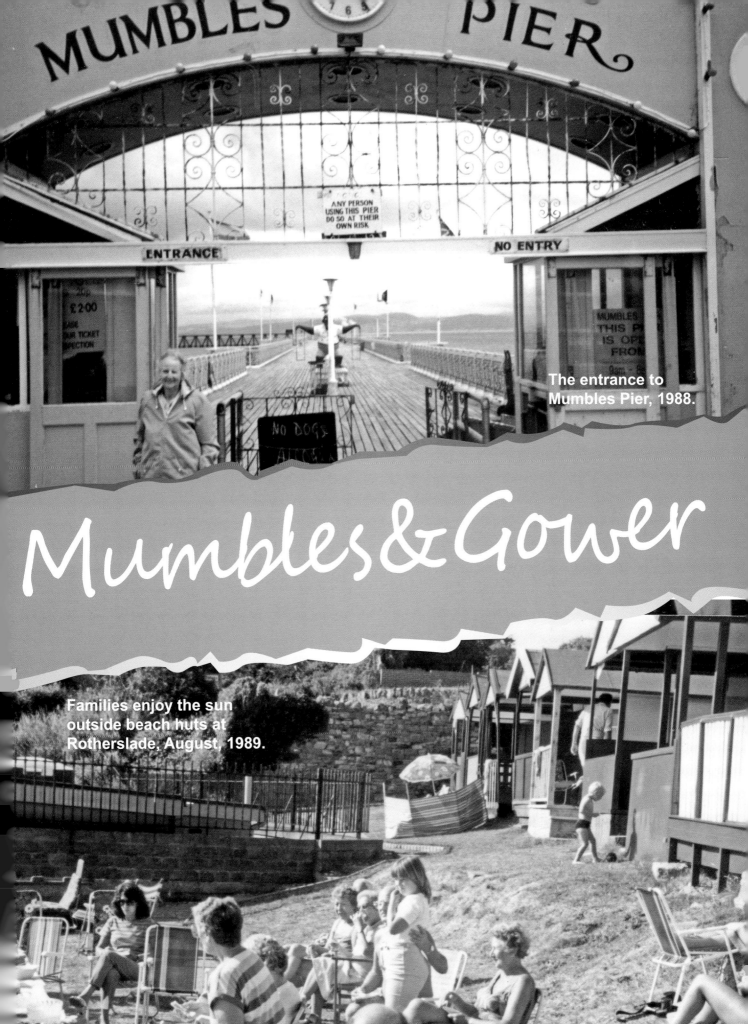

MUMBLES PIER

ANY PERSON USING THIS PIER DO SO AT THEIR OWN RISK

ENTRANCE

NO ENTRY

NO DOGS

The entrance to Mumbles Pier, 1988.

Mumbles & Gower

Families enjoy the sun outside beach huts at Rotherslade, August, 1989.

A view of Oystermouth, 1903. The property set back from the roadway in the centre is The George Hotel.

The Bishopston Valley Hotel, Bishopston, 1910.

The exterior of the Mermaid Hotel, Mumbles, and below, its equally impressive dining room, 1903.

Mumbles Pier showing the tea gardens, 1920.

The end of Mumbles Pier, mid-1980s.

A low tide view of the pier showing its main supports, early 1970s.

Mumbles Pier closed for refurbishment in July 2011. The images on this page will be a reminder of how it has appeared down the decades. The main picture shows the pier and amusement arcade in 1969.

Mumbles Pier and lifeboat house, mid-1980s.

The Osborne Hotel, beach and tea rooms, Rotherslade, 1912.

Looking over the car park at Bracelet Bay towards Mumbles lighthouse, mid-1930s.

The first stand at the Gower Show of Swansea company FG Trew & Son Ltd, 1968. In those days the company traded as builders merchants and ironmongers. Today, the long established company is still based in King Edward Road, but now specialises in plumbing, bathrooms and renewable energy systems.

The castellated facade of Kilvrough Manor, Gower, 1972.

A cigarette machine opposite the park at Southend, 1975. They were once a familiar sight.

Cottages alongside the ford at Parkmill, Gower, mid-1970s.

Looking down over Cheriton, North Gower, September 1975. Burry Port and the old Carmarthen Bay power station are in the distance.

Looking down Newton Road, Mumbles, and across Swansea Bay towards Port Talbot, October 1981.

Rotherslade, with its shelter and beach huts, mid-1980s. The Osborne Hotel is on the left.
Both the shelter and the Osborne have since been demolished.

The majestic sweep of Langland Bay with the golf course in the distance, 1988.

A view of Oystermouth Castle, from Castle Street, Mumbles, 1980s.

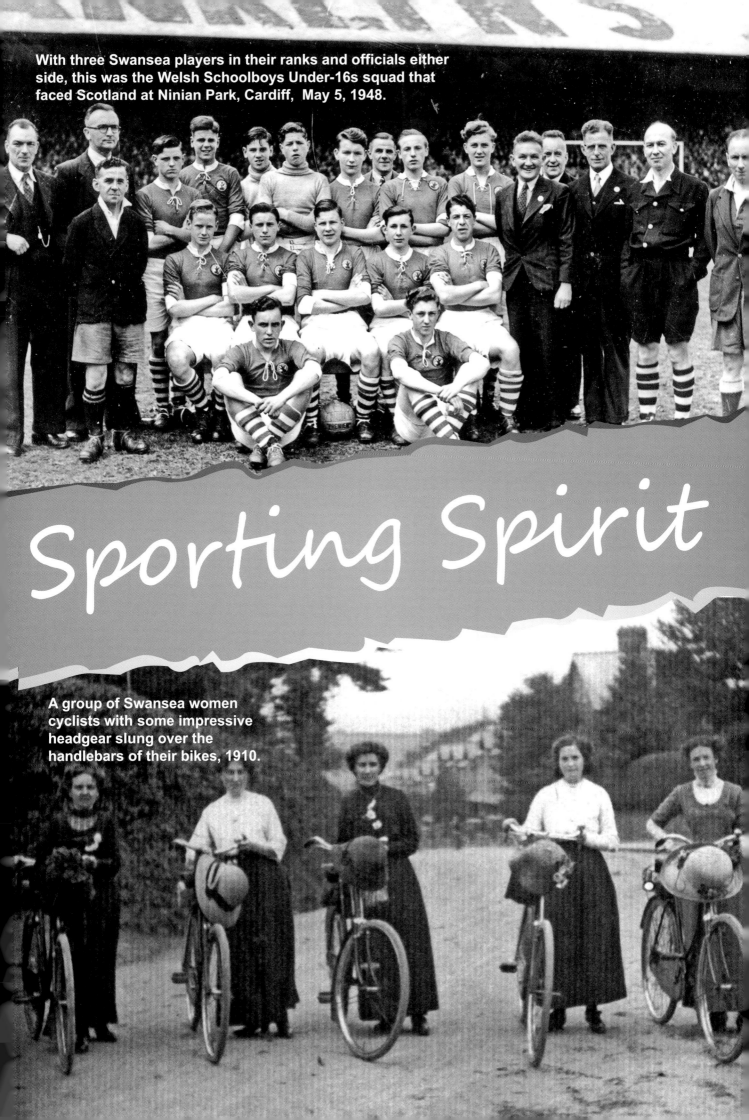

With three Swansea players in their ranks and officials either side, this was the Welsh Schoolboys Under-16s squad that faced Scotland at Ninian Park, Cardiff, May 5, 1948.

Sporting Spirit

A group of Swansea women cyclists with some impressive headgear slung over the handlebars of their bikes, 1910.

Members and officials of Pontardawe Hockey Club, late 1890s.

Swansea Senior League team Winch Wen AFC, mid-1950s.

The Swansea Schoolboys football team which played Mountain Ash in January, 1947.

Swansea's Brunswick AFC on their Easter tour to Dublin, 1949.

A gathering of Swansea Schoolboys who attained their caps for Wales between 1948 and 1958.

A jubilant Port Tennant Stars team, with officials, at the Vetch Field, 1955. The club were Swansea Senior League Cup finalists for six years running.

Officials of Cwm Albion AFC with impressive trophies won in a successful season, early 1950s.

A Bishop Gore School soccer team, 1956-57 season.

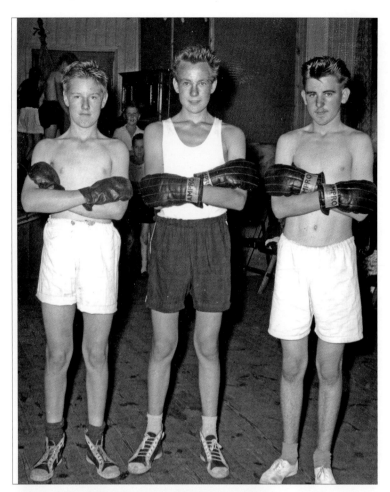

Three young members of
Swansea British Railways
Boxing Club, 1957.

Bishop Gore Grammar School's
under-15s cricket XI who were
Swansea Schools champions, 1953.

Two Swansea snooker players celebrate with their friends after success in the Note Doubles Championship, 1967.

A combination of women's darts team members from the Shipping Inn, Sloane Street, and Paxton Hotel, Paxton Street, 1966.

Kilvey Athletic football team, runners-up against Llanelly Steel in the West Wales Senior Cup final, 1964. They lost 4-0.

Members of the darts team of the Prince of Wales public house, Mumbles, celebrating winning the Gower Darts League, mid-1960s.

Swansea Town captain Mike Johnson shakes the hand of his opposite number on a rain soaked Villa Park pitch before the Swans' FA Cup semi-final against Preston, 1964.

A solitary moment of jubilation after Swansea Town's Jimmy McLaughlin scores in the FA Cup semi-final against Preston North End, 1964. The final score was 2-1 to Preston.

Members of Bonymaen Athletic Football Club during a tour of London, 1959.

The Swansea Sunday League football team of the Bay View Hotel, Oystermouth Road, 1979.

Successful members of the St Illtyd's Club, Port Tennant, women's darts team with trophies they scooped during a successful season of competition, 1972.

Sketty Park Colts get a team talk from coach Tommy Crabbe, 1968.

Members and officials of Kilvey Athletic football team on a tour of Jersey, 1969.

Members of Swansea's Paxton United who played against Millwall in a testimonial for Millwall captain Barry Kitchener, 1976. The game, played at Dartford Football Club, was drawn 5-5.

Swansea's It's a Knockout team after winning the British heat that was held at St Helen's sports ground, 1975.

The Swansea Schools Cricket Association team at Pentrehafod School, 1982.

Members of the under-11s team at St Joseph's School, Greenhill, 1986.

Swans star Alan Curtis controls the ball under the watchful eye of experienced Arsenal defender David O'Leary at the Vetch Field during Swansea City's glorious First Division days, 1981.

Swansea Docks engineering department's football team at Landore, 1985.

Swansea City right-back Neil Robinson on the attack in Swansea's First Division home game against Arsenal, 1981.

Goal scorers Alan Curtis and Bob Latchford celebrate as the Swans beat Leeds United 5-1 at the Vetch Field on the opening day of the 1981-82 season in the old First Division.

Celebrating promotion to the old First Division after the 3-1 win at Preston on May 2, 1981, are Swansea legends (from left) Alan Curtis, Jeremy Charles and Robbie James.

Olchfa School netball team, 1981.

The netball team of Olchfa School with teacher Beverley Jones, late 1984.

Members of the St Illtyd's ladies' darts team from Port Tennant, 1984.

The Hafod Primary School football team, 1982-83.

187

The North End football team which took part in the BSC Velindre works Reserve Cup Final, 1980.

The netball team at Brynhyfryd Junior School, 1983.

The class of 81. Some of the victorious Swansea City team that clinched promotion to the old First Division in 1981 were reunited at the Liberty Stadium many years later. They are, from left: John Toshack, manager; Malcolm Struel, chairman; Nigel Stevenson, Wyndham Evans, Alan Curtis, Dave Stewart, Leighton Phillips and Leighton James.

St Joseph's School Colts Under-9s team with trainers Gary Jones and Bryn Rees, 1982.

Action men: Midfielder Mark Gower, above, and striker Stephen Dobbie, below, shoot at goal during the 2010-11 season as Swansea City won promotion to the Premier League, the most watched football league in the world.

What a way to close this book. When it comes to nostalgia this picture already says it all. Few will forget the magical moment when Swansea City manager Brendan Rodgers hoisted the npower Championship play-off trophy in the air after his club's historic 4-2 win over Reading at Wembley, May 30, 2011. It made them the first ever Welsh club to play in the Premier League, a landmark for both the club and the city.

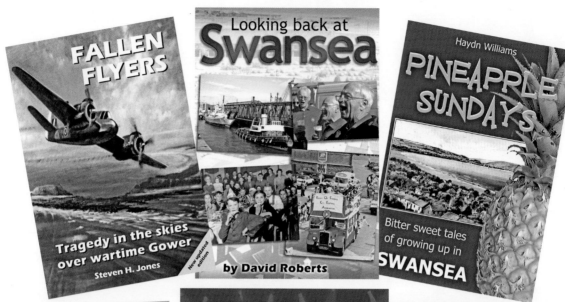
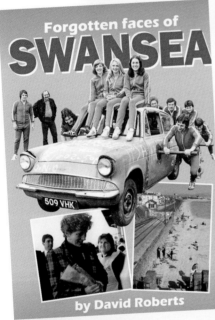
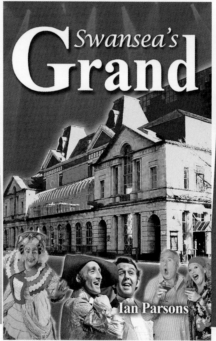
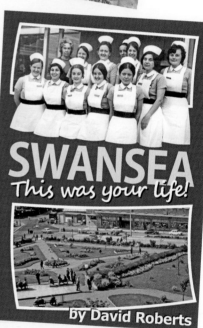
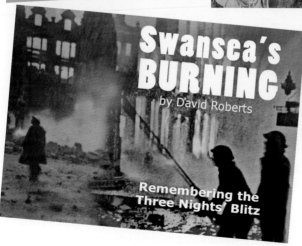
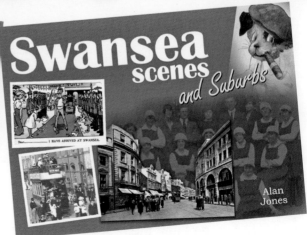